Mindful thoughts for
WALKERS

First published in the UK and North America in 2017 by

Leaping Hare Press

An imprint of The Quarto Group
The Old Brewery, 6 Blundell Street
London N7 9BH, United Kingdom
T (0)20 7700 6700 **F** (0)20 7700 8066
www.QuartoKnows.com

British Library Cataloguing-in-Publication Data
A catalogue record for this book is available from the British Library

ISBN: 978-1-78240-484-2

This book was conceived, designed and produced by

Leaping Hare Press

58 West Street, Brighton BN1 2RA, UK

Publisher: *Susan Kelly*
Creative Director: *Michael Whitehead*
Editorial Director: *Tom Kitch*
Art Director: *James Lawrence*
Commissioning Editor: *Monica Perdoni*
Editor: *Jenni Davis*
Assistant Editor: *Jenny Campbell*
Designer: *Tina Smith*
Illustrator: *Lehel Kovacs*

Printed in China

7 9 10 8

Mindful thoughts for

WALKERS

Footnotes on the zen path

Adam Ford

Leaping Hare Press

Contents

Walking the
Buddhist Path

One of the kindest things we can do for ourselves is to go for a good walk. It is one of the most natural activities in the world, exercising the body and stimulating the heart, while at the same time freeing the mind to become more open and alert. Like an over-tight muscle, the mind needs to be loosened before it can let go, so we are then able to enjoy the present moment and face reality. We return from a successful walk refreshed and clear-headed.

The purpose of this book is to explore how we may use walking as a way to increase our levels of awareness and to improve our conscious living – to make the walk more enjoyable as we come to understand our place in the world of nature. The questions that lurk at the back of the mind can be faced: Who am I? Where have I come from? Where am I going? The walking may involve no more than a daily gentle stroll, or it may extend to that well-planned great hike that takes us beyond the horizon, following the course of a great river, or over mountain ranges and through remote forests.

Mindfulness is a way to keep in touch with reality, important for each of us individually, but also as members of a powerful and potentially destructive species. As an exercise, it has its roots both in human nature and in Buddhism. It is not always easy to be a human being; increasingly, we are in danger of living lives of fevered anxiety, concerned about the past and worried about the future, forgetting the life that is to be found here and now. We feel that in growing older we have lost something, that innocent ability in childhood to take unquestioning delight in simple things – a ladybird, a toy or a gift.

Two and a half thousand years ago, the Buddha incorporated mindfulness into his teaching as a major element in the Eightfold Path and the perennial fight against ignorance. He encouraged his followers to become more attentive to their bodies, their feelings and their thoughts; to get to know and understand that bundle of worries that threatens to spoil life; to become more aware. He lived at a time of great change, when the old religions were being questioned, and taught a new spiritual way to explore life, one that was available to anyone, whatever their caste and whether they were religious or not.

An early image of the Buddha shows him sitting; one hand trails forward and is in touch with the ground. The original story is that the Buddha made a vow in a previous life to achieve enlightenment; in touching the ground, he is calling the earth to bear witness to the vow. He is meditating, but that does not mean he is away somewhere in the mind palace of his own head – he is earthed like a lightning conductor to physical reality, to the present moment in the material and spiritual world.

One well-trodden way to practise mindfulness is to go for a good walk and to follow the Buddha's simple advice: 'When walking – just walk.'

The Burden
of Me

The Buddha taught mindfulness as part of the Eightfold Path, the Buddhist way of life, but it is just as valuable as a practice when separated from its religious origins. In a sense, mindfulness is no more Buddhist than the principles of loving-kindness or forgiveness are exclusively Christian.

The Buddha was aware that life in the sixth century BCE was full of problems, pain and suffering; apart from anything else, we all face old age, disease and death. The majority of people he observed were ill at ease with themselves and in need of guidance on how best to live their lives. Emotional ignorance about what it means to be a human being was as widespread then as it is today.

Traditional religion in his time was dominated by the divisive caste system, people allocated at birth to their place in a hierarchical society, and by a powerful priesthood who controlled the worship and festivals of the era. The Buddha wanted to give people something else; he offered them a path to follow that would not depend on any social system or priesthood but one in which they would be responsible for their own spiritual progress. 'Work out your own salvation with diligence' were his last words to a friend.

The fundamental problem he identified is that of 'me'. Each of us clings to an inflamed sense of self, a misguided focus, he believed, which is the cause of much of our pain. This comes as a challenging thought to Westerners who have grown up in a culture that lauds the individual, applauds self-confidence and bolsters the ego. We admire great personalities and reward them with continuous press coverage. But perhaps we have grown accustomed to thinking of the self in the wrong sort of way.

LEARNING TO ACCEPT WHO WE ARE

Who is it that is walking? We may be coping with
negative feelings about ourselves, who we are and the
way we have behaved, with memories that make us
wince and worries that undermine us. But our feelings
and thoughts come and go like storm clouds and it can
be a great relief to realize that none of them are 'me'.

Most of us will not want to go as far as the Buddha
in this self-analysis, for he concluded that having stripped
away everything, there is no such thing as the self (his
goal was the remote and wordless state of bliss known
as Nirvana). In the terms of modern neuroscience he
would describe the self as a 'construct', an invention of
the brain working to hold together all of our experience
in a meaningful way. The eighteenth-century Scottish
philosopher David Hume observed something similar,
describing the human being as merely a bundle of
sensations: 'For my part, when I enter most intimately
into what I call myself, I always stumble on some
particular perception or other, of heat or cold, light

or shade, love or hatred, pain or pleasure. I never can catch myself at any time without a perception, and never can observe anything but the perception.'

Whatever our view on the nature of 'me' – and we may prefer the language of soul when talking about our inner selves – the Buddhist approach at least suggests that we can let go many of the things in our self-image that torment us; we have more inner freedom than we realized. We learn to accept who we are.

LET GO OF THINKING

Going for a good walk is a great way of letting go the burden of 'me'. It gives us rhythmical time for sorting out our thoughts; for coming to terms with our humanity – mortal, afflicted with doubt and feelings of guilt, vulnerable and often clouded by confusion. This does not mean that we walk away from our problems; it is more a case of getting them in proportion, seeing them for what they are and not allowing them to dominate us with guilt, worry or anxiety.

Here we must be careful, because when walking mindfully we should just walk, and rather than struggle with our various burdens, our first challenge is to let go of thinking. Just walk, one foot after the other. Later, things will begin to sort themselves out naturally, without effort. Let the head and the heart become clear without agonizing. Begin to look outwards; notice the sounds around you, the cooing of a pigeon or the whir of farm machinery in the distance; acknowledge the passer-by with a nod or a smile; stop and watch the flight of a butterfly. Consciously breathe the air and feel it giving life to the body.

Tramping
Old Tracks

Ancient human tracks cover the planet; many are barely
recognizable, now either overgrown or transformed into
highways. Some mark the long and lonely links between
remote settlements, while others record a dense web of
hunting, pilgrimage and travel – a revealing map of human
social history etched into the ground, worn down by
foot, hoof and wheel. Old trade routes span the world:
the Silk Road from China, flowing with spices, cloth and
porcelain; the north–south trails that saw the movement
of scarlet macaws from Mexico traded for turquoise
from Arizona; the migrant wanderings of pioneers
moving west across North America or the Aborigine
songlines tracking the Dreamtime peopling of Australia.

A little local research will reveal what old ways are available to you for a mindful walk of a different nature. Many people will be familiar with the lovely poem by Rudyard Kipling, *The Way through the Woods*. It begins:

They shut the road through the woods
Seventy years ago.
Weather and rain have undone it again,
And now you would never know
There was once a road through the woods.

Then Kipling's imagination is stirred by the thought of who may have passed that way long ago and he continues, later in the poem:

Yet, if you enter the woods
Of a summer evening late,
When the night-air cools on the trout-ringed pools…
You will hear the beat of a horse's feet
And the swish of a skirt in the dew,…

WALKING IN THE COMPANY OF SPIRITS

This is the fascination of old tracks and trails – the thought of all the people who have travelled that way, carrying their loads, both real and metaphorical. By walking these paths, we join a company of spirits, sharing with them the same views of the passing horizon, resting on the same rocks, sometimes even seeking the shade of the same ancient wayside trees.

When walking along an ancient track, it will sometimes take a bit of detective work to recognize the telltale signs of age and usage, the way well-worn from the passage of people going about their business for many generations. A good map will indicate the route of an old Roman road, cutting, in military style, straight across the landscape through fields, down newer lanes and through woodland. Many maps will show clearly the track of an old coach road worth exploring for its quietness, running roughly parallel to the new motorway that has replaced it. But many minor tracks, often hundreds of years old, will only appear as bridleways or footpaths, with no hint of their venerable age.

In mountainous wooded areas where farmers have traditionally taken their cattle up on to high rich pastures in the spring and herded them back down to the valleys for winter, the regular tracks they use can be easy to identify. They meander down through the forest, often bordered by ancient and roughly built stone walls, where gnarled and twisted trees took root centuries ago; they skirt huge boulders, cross streams where they are shallow and, if still in use, are churned up with dead leaves and mud. To walk these tracks is to walk into a world of the past.

ADDING OUR OWN FOOTPRINTS

When a country path on hard ground crosses bare rock, the wheels of carts have sometimes scarred the track with grooves, making our own footprints seem incredibly transient and ephemeral in comparison.

And if your walk takes you up across high open moorland, through heather, cotton grass and bracken, you may find the way marked by lichen-covered rocks, rolled into place in a long-past era; now they are almost lost in tussocks of sedge and mounds of moss. Some of these ancient paths date back thousands of years to the days of the first Neolithic farmers. One can only wonder what the people who first used them would think of the world we live in now.

But it is the sunken paths, the 'hollow ways', that we may find most mysterious, the old routes and coach roads ridden and tramped for so many centuries that they have dug deep into the ground, with banks so high that the walker is lost in a tunnel of vegetation, badger sets and the ivy-covered trunks of fallen trees flanking the path. Woodpeckers fly off noisily and flocks of small birds hawk through the canopy above. Walking here, we have a real sense of hiking through history, of sharing the way with ghosts of the past – and realizing that for future generations, we will be part of their number.

The Illusion
of Haste

'Don't rush! If we miss this bus, we can catch the next one!'

An older man was speaking to a slightly younger one, both retired from full-time employment. They were setting off for a long walk over local hill country, on a bright autumn morning. The younger man felt momentarily reprimanded for his haste in wanting to get on with the day, to attack the track. Then he recognized that his companion was right. There was no need to rush. The time did not matter.

Rushing about seems to characterize the twenty-first century. We live in a fast-moving world, always filling the time, wanting to get things done. We forget how to stop and stand still, ignoring that old, often irritating aphorism 'more haste, less speed' – irritating because it only ever seems to be mentioned by some critical observer when we have made a mess of things.

The need to learn how to stop and stand still is essential for our spiritual health, and it is something we can practise when walking. A lot depends on age and fitness, of course, and it is certainly important, when walking for exercise, to get the heart beating a bit faster, the breathing deeper, to fill the lungs with oxygen, to get the blood moving around your body. We all know the pleasure that comes from a good workout, one that we found challenging, causing us to break out in a healthy sweat. But there are also times when we will benefit from learning how to stop.

BACK ON THE MINDFUL TRACK

We may have accelerated into a walking rhythm faster than we had intended, driven by some inner demon, forgetting to be mindful of the moment. Or, if we are

24

an older person, we may be driving ourselves too hard, turning the hill into a challenge to be conquered rather than enjoyed. Everything in us conspires to make us press ahead, eyes glued to the path, perhaps even muttering with the strain, oblivious to the beautiful landscape around. Pride, and a habit of haste, the desire to 'get it done', are all rolled into one. Then, with luck, we may come to our senses and realize how ridiculous we have become – and stop. Our fretful thinking has dominated our actions, prompting us to feel driven. Two minutes spent breathing consciously, aware of the in-breath and the out-breath in mindfulness fashion, and we are back on the mindful track.

I recently relearnt this lesson myself, once again – it is easy to forget! I was fell-walking with family; our aim was to get to the top of a local peak, one I hadn't climbed in years. But I am getting older and walking uphill is getting tougher year by year. Could I do it, I wondered? It took a great effort of self-control to slow down and adopt a different, more relaxed rhythm than the younger members of the party. My young niece kept running ahead; she would sit on a rock far above and grin, then make off again when we reached her. She was very gracious about it, never once saying 'Hurry up!' or joking about my slower progress.

LEARN HOW TO BE STILL

Learning to slow down, and even to stop, is not just a matter of breaking the journey when climbing a hill; once we have discovered how to stop, it becomes an inner attitude that can accompany our actions as well as arresting them.

There is a story told of the Buddha to this effect in the early sutras. A gruesome highwayman, with a fetish for collecting human fingers, which he wore as a necklace, followed the Buddha into the forest. His name was Angulimala (meaning 'finger garland'). A local king wanted the loathsome robber captured and, knowing this, the Buddha had set out to find him, letting himself be the bait. When Angulimala saw the Buddha he drew his sword and rushed after him, lusting after just one more finger for his grisly collection. But the Buddha just kept quietly walking on, unconcerned, unflustered. Angulimala ran faster, breaking into a sweat – but still, however fast he ran he could not catch up with the gently walking Buddha. Finally, the robber collapsed on the ground, exhausted.

Turning to him, the Buddha said, 'Angulimala – I stopped long ago. It is time for you to give up your violent ways and learn how to be still.' Angulimala was immediately enlightened, letting go his inner demons. He became a devoted and mindful follower of the Buddha.

Taking Time
to Breathe

The thing to remember about mindfulness is that it is completely natural, something we often practise without even trying. When alert and absorbed in weeding the garden, cooking a meal, painting a picture or enjoying the fresh air and landscape on a country walk, we may already be in a mindful state – consciously involved, here and now, in a fulfilling activity. Such moments may be rare in our daily lives, for our living experience is often cluttered with a background noise of worries and anxieties, self-doubts, stress and uncertainties – but those moments do not have to be rare. By recognizing and savouring the quality of mindfulness, we can learn to foster it and live in peace in the present moment, anywhere.

The principal mindfulness exercise involves our breathing. We depend for our existence upon the invisible life-giving oxygen in the air – five minutes or so without breathing and we are dead, and yet most of the time we give it such little thought. For this exercise, we should be comfortable, standing or sitting, holding the back straight but without strain, not slumped, and with the shoulders open. Nothing should be forced; breathe gently and our bodies will tell us how much air we need. Then we simply watch our breathing, feeling the in-breath as the air flows in, opening our lungs, following the out-breath as our lungs deflate. By focusing on this simple activity, we find that our mind has stopped roaming about and our bodies begin to experience calm.

FINDING OUR RHYTHM

We can also practise mindfulness while walking, coordinating our breathing with the regular swing of our limbs. Again, nothing should be forced; simply get into a comfortable rhythm and become aware of how the breath comes and goes. We are all built differently and have to find our own way into what instinctively feels right and easy. The Zen Buddhist master Thich Nhat Hanh has some recommendations in his little book *How to Walk* that may be helpful to some readers; he considers how to enjoy walking through crowds in a busy city or in an airport, how to climb stairs. He suggests that we should begin by taking two steps for the in-breath and three steps for the out-breath – or, if we find it easier, three steps and five steps. The numbers will be reduced when climbing a hill. We listen to our bodies and adapt, each of us finding our own natural rhythm.

Mindful breathing and mindful walking are the basis for our further exploration of the way in which we relate to the world we inhabit and, contemplate our place in the living ecosystem, our connections to other creatures. We feel the earth beneath our feet and the steady pull of the gravity of the planet – particularly when toiling uphill. By becoming more aware of our bodies in the present moment, we have located a strong place from which to become more conscious and appreciative of our surroundings.

LEARN TO REMEMBER

The French writer, activist and philosopher Simone Weil once wrote that all scientific research is a form of religious contemplation, and while we do not set out on a walk with the disciplines of science in mind, we can, in our own ways, be researching the reality of the world at our own level. When following a long trail, walking from horizon to horizon, by observing the landscape passing by, fields and hedgerows, buildings, meandering streams, rushing rivers or outcrops of rock, we can be learning to recognize those features that are man-made and those that are natural. We become more mindful of the geography of our home planet and the ways in which our species has altered, and is continuing to alter, its surface.

We will be guided by our own interests – in birds or butterflies, perhaps, or flowering plants or trees. Learning to identify them is a way to notice in more detail the rich nature of the ecosystem of which we are part. It is only when one comes to look closely at a butterfly to determine its species, for example, that we begin to register the beautiful colours of its wings or the delicate markings on its underside. It is only when we have learned to stand still and listen that we begin to distinguish the song of a wren from a robin, or of a thrush from a blackbird.

Once we have discovered the joy and calm that can come with mindfulness, we should not forget, but learn to remember and foster it when we return from the walk to the family, the office or the city. It will help carry us through stress, anxiety or worry.

Inhaling
Knowledge

You walk through woodland in the spring, perhaps along a winding path made by a badger, when suddenly you catch the scent of garlic – wild garlic. You stop and look about you and there, beneath the bushes and around the fallen timber and old decaying tree stumps, white flowers are bursting from a carpet of fresh, glossy green leaves. You have caught the scent and you breathe it in. Savour it: the wild scents of nature are elusive; we have forgotten how to enjoy them.

Why should dogs have all the fun? Their excitement is palpable as they rush about a new hedgerow or field, nose to the ground, clearly overwhelmed and intoxicated by all that is on offer. The trail of a fox or a cat requires investigation; the scent of a rabbit or a mouse gets the juices flowing. As for lamp posts…! There are scents and smells available to a dog beyond the imagination or dreams of human beings.

CATCHING THE ELUSIVE SCENT

The practice of mindfulness begins by focusing on the breath; for the moment, you let go of any tormenting baggage in the mind – anxious thoughts from yesterday, nagging worries about tomorrow – and relax into the body and its life-giving breath. You let the in-breath gently fill the lungs, hold it for a moment and then allow it to flow out again. You do it in your own time and to your own rhythm, without forcing the air either way. In this way, we begin to be more alert, awake and aware.

And with the breath comes that elusive scent. Sniff too hard and it escapes you; wait, breathe gently and you may catch it again. The olfactory system is one of the oldest sensory parts of the brain, evolved in mammals to help in the detection of food and the discernment of poison (how clever of evolution to locate the nose so close to the mouth!). For most of us, however, it has become a deadened sense; we don't rely on it for any useful information, and apart from the delight that comes with the first smell of the morning's coffee or the disgust with the traffic fumes of the city, we neglect what it has to tell us.

Despite this elusiveness, there are smells that momentarily overpower us with memory. The smell of tar takes us back to the garden gate when we were three years old, watching men mend the road; the smell of new-mown hay transports us to happy summers in childhood. We step into the carriage of a train and are suddenly transported we know not where by the faintest of smells: 'I have been here before! When? Where was I when I last caught that familiar, but long forgotten, odour?' The timelessness of the experience can be very strange as we search in our thoughts to locate its origins. Then it is gone, lost perhaps like a hint of honeysuckle on the night air. We are left wondering.

RESOLVE TO SNIFF

It is an aspect of mindfulness to become more aware of the scents that assail us as we walk; we may make a resolution as we set off some morning to detect and entertain them, rather than noticing anything else. Stroll through a city and the smells, both artificial and real, that waft from fishmongers or cafés, soap shops or those selling leather goods, can be overwhelming as they mix with the fumes of vehicles, and the perfumes and aftershaves of passing pedestrians. For more subtle and perennial scents, we need to get outdoors in the countryside. Walk across heathland and you may be lucky enough to catch the coconut scent of yellow gorse, almost suffocating on a warm day; dip down into a marshy hollow and find the distinctive odour of bog myrtle.

THE SCENT OF AUTUMN

Perhaps the most evocative smells of the countryside come to us in the autumn. They are worth holding at the centre of our awareness with a gentle intake of breath through the nostrils, as though catching the bouquet of an untried wine; it helps to shut the eyes. In the orchard there is the fruity scent of apples and pears, while down in the woods the powerful stench of a stinkhorn toadstool catches our attention, or the rich aroma of decaying wood and of rotting vegetation, the humus. It is worth reminding ourselves that the word 'humus' shares the same Indo-European root as the words human, humour and humility. We, as we walk testing the air, are products of the rich soil, part of the biological cycle. Decay fuels life.

The Zen Bell of
Enlightenment

Try listening to your surroundings for a change, rather than looking at them. Most of us, when walking, rely more on our eyes than we do on our ears; our 'picture' of the landscape is visual. But it can be rewarding sometimes to turn down the dimmer switch on sight and turn up the volume on sound. This is a very useful mindfulness exercise, improving our level of awareness, immersing us in the present moment.

Go for a walk and just listen. You may need to half-close your eyes (be careful not to wander into the sea if on a beach or tumble off a mountain track!). It may even be better and less hazardous to take a pause from the walking and sit on a seat or stand by a gatepost, until you become accustomed to listening. Much of the time we block the sounds of the world around us; we have learned to shut them out as irritating interruptions to what we are doing. Now, let them into your conscious mind and you may be astonished by all there is to hear. Listen attentively, as a child does when absorbed and enthralled by the apparent distant roar of the ocean in a seashell held to the ear.

JUST LISTEN

Sounds have a long-standing part to play in Buddhist meditation – the Tibetan temple bell, for instance, echoing the impermanence of things – while in Zen the clear sound of a bell can be the vehicle of enlightenment, awakening the mind to its true nature, bringing the meditating monk or nun into the present moment. But these 'enlightenment' experiences are rare and not to be expected or grasped at. In fact, don't expect anything as you listen; just listen. The expectations of mindfulness are gentle, simply opening mental windows to let in fresh air. They are akin to an older tradition than Zen, the Way of Tao. There we learn that although you may hear a cockerel crow in a neighbouring village, there is no need to go there – be content with where you are, here and now.

THE MINDFULNESS OF THE BLIND

The fully sighted among us are beginners in the art of listening compared to those who are permanently blind; they have refined their ability to survey their surroundings through sound. They can 'hear' the lamp post as they approach it, from the echoes of their footfall; they can explore a room and its furniture by snapping their fingers and listening to the way the sound bounces off soft furnishings or blank walls; they can confidently cross roads at major junctions by recognizing the noisy ebb and flow of traffic as it stops and starts at traffic lights. Their abilities make us realize that there is a world out there waiting to be explored.

When walking through open country, there is often so much to listen to. I recollect a colleague of mine, years ago, telling me how he learned to be more attuned and alert to nature by sharing walking holidays with a blind cousin. His companion would stop, point at the sky and say 'John – buzzards mewing!' and there, high above them, a pair of buzzards would be circling on a thermal beneath a cumulus cloud. 'I would never have noticed,' said John.

THE LUXURY OF LISTENING

We don't often allow ourselves the luxury of listening to the sound of wind stirring through the treetops. When the wind blows, every tree has its own signature sound. The wind sings in an isolated thorn bush as you walk by; the deep rustle of an oak tree is different from the gentle soughing of a fir, or the agitated shaking of an aspen. On a blustery day, you can listen to the way the wind moves through a wood or makes its way up a valley; watch the trees bend and wave as it comes towards you, then wait for the movement of the next gust. The same is true of the rain as it sweeps across a cabbage field – the swish of distant pattering becomes a roar as it approaches and passes by. Listening, you follow its retreat across country.

Some sounds stick with you; the liquid call of a curlew on open moorland or out on an estuary can lift you out of yourself and maybe transport you back to an earlier memory; the full-throated song of a thrush or a mockingbird break through a sadness that has been shrouding you perhaps for weeks, with all the power of enlightenment of a Zen bell, lifting your spirits, proclaiming new life.

The
Forest Walk

Trees were growing on the planet, pumping moisture into the atmosphere, breathing out oxygen, stirred by the wind in early dawns, long before we were here to see them. They saw the dinosaurs come and go, witnessed the appearance of the first flowering plants, and laid down the great coal deposits that fuelled the Industrial Revolution. Individually, they can live for many hundreds of years. Walk among trees and you share the air and the light with some of the oldest living beings on Earth.

There is strong evidence that walking in a forest is good for human health. Research in Japan suggests that two or three days spent holidaying in a forest, a practice called *Shinrin-yoku* or 'forest bathing', boosts the human immune system. The theory supporting the claim is that by immersing oneself in a forest one is exposed to airborne chemicals that plants release to protect themselves against rotting and insects. Whatever the strength of this claim, I myself can vouch for the fact that I always return from walking among trees refreshed and with a sense of well-being. Perhaps there is some truth in those words of an Indian mystic: 'Be still – for each tree is a silent prayer.'

A THREE-DIMENSIONAL EXPERIENCE

Some of the pleasure of walking in a forest is the way it demands that you look about you in every direction, peering up, down, around and deep into its depths – not because it is scary, but because it is a three-dimensional experience. The canopy above your head is as interesting as the ground beneath your feet; the undergrowth and ferns close by the path are as eye-catching as the trunks of the trees. Stands of straight timber, like the pillars of a great cathedral, reveal intriguing caverns of space, dark and mysterious. The walker can't help looking between and beyond the brush, the branches and the trunks, probing the half-light and the shadows.

One instinctively walks slowly through a wood or forest, as though venturing on to hallowed ground. There is so much to take in, the senses alerted from every direction – the smell of loam and rotting leaves, the noisy clatter of a wood pigeon flying off, the crackle of broken twigs as some startled creature, glimpsed for a moment in the dappled light, disappears into the dense undergrowth.

Find a place to stop. Get intimate. Feel the texture of a tree trunk, the smooth flanks of a beech or the rough, spongy and punchable bark of a redwood. Breathe deeply and inhale the smell of the humus on the forest floor. If possible, find a place to sit, a log perhaps, or if you are lucky and you are walking the forest path in a park, there may be a bench. This would be a good spot to do the mindful breathing exercise (see pages 28–33).

Take time. Recognize any distracting or troubling thoughts you may have; acknowledge them and let them go. Focus on the air as you inhale slowly, opening your lungs then exhaling without effort. Become aware of yourself as a breathing body sitting among trees.

LOOK AND LEARN

Notice the quietness, and all those sounds of the forest that enhance the silence: wind in the treetops, branches rubbing together, the twittering of birds foraging for insects. When your spirit is settled, begin to look around you, identifying the trees, remembering that learning the names is a way of noticing: the oak, the ash, the pine, the straight-logged poplar. It will, of course, depend on where you are, and the more you treat yourself to forest walking, the more varieties of tree you will come to see and recognize. You may then have the thrill one day of entering a forest where everything is new to you; perhaps you are visiting a country overseas, where the trees create a totally new arboreal experience.

It is only when you stop and really look that you begin to see colours you might not have expected. We tend to assume that tree trunks are grey or brown – full stop. Attend to them more closely and we find a richer palate than we had imagined: russet red in the pine; blue in the ash; white in the birch and purple-brown in the dead wood. Lichens add smears of burnt orange, yellow, blue and grey. The patterns and colours on the trunks of eucalypts can be as abstract as the painting of a modern artist. A shaft of sunlight illuminating the vibrant green of moss on a trunk can be momentarily astonishing.

The
Pilgrim Way

Do we need a goal when going for a walk? In one sense the answer has to be no, because when walking mindfully the purpose is simply to walk, letting go of concerns about either past or future – relaxing through the steady rhythm of walking, becoming more aware of the present moment through breathing consciously.

And yet there are times when having a goal and purpose can be a help. A pilgrimage provides such a goal. Traditionally, the pilgrim way has been associated with prayer, adoration, healing and hope. The Muslim going to Mecca for the Hajj will whisper 'Lord, here I come'; the Christian tramping the medieval Camino pilgrimage route to Santiago de Compostela may address prayers to St James the Apostle, asking for his intercession; the Hindu walking the length of the Ganges offers his journey as an act of adoration to his god. The activity of walking is a deeply satisfying way of involving the whole body in prayer.

But not all pilgrimage requires belief in God. Many who practise walking mindfully do not hold any particular religious belief at all. It has even been argued that the Buddha, who taught mindfulness as part of his Way, was himself an atheist; he offered a spiritual path towards understanding the nature of life, dispensing with the many gods of his day.

CREATE YOUR OWN PILGRIMAGE

Your pilgrimage could be to a much loved view, or, like the New England writer Henry David Thoreau, a favourite tree. In *Walden: or, Life in the Woods*, Thoreau records how he walked ten miles through snow one winter to keep an appointment with a beech tree, to be in its presence. For me, a short uphill walk takes me, in all weathers, to a gate from where I can see the sea, stand for a moment to catch my breath and enjoy just being there. The tree, the gatepost, the view – they all offer a focus, a goal for the walk, an added pleasure and satisfaction. Each in its own way is a pilgrimage.

Let us not draw heavy lines between what is religious and what is not. Primarily we are human beings, heirs to many religious cultures, each offering its own practices and ways to understand and live our lives. Everyone, whatever their faith or belief system, can benefit from, and enjoy, walking a traditional pilgrimage route, whether it be to the sanctuary of a saint, a mountain or a holy well. When we walk, we are enjoying a spiritual activity wisely fostered by all the great religions of the world.

THE PILGRIMAGE WALK

There is currently a resurgent interest in the pilgrimage walk, combining physical with spiritual pleasure. These hikes are not only to the great traditional centres of pilgrimage – many are newly created, following minor paths to local churches. Their purpose is to encourage a mindful attitude to walking and a cool quiet place to sit and think at the end of the journey. We can even create our own personal pilgrimage route, perhaps a circular one, near to home.

The focus for medieval pilgrims travelling to the English city of Canterbury was the tomb of the martyred saint Thomas Becket, murdered in the cathedral in 1170. The culmination of the journey would be to touch or kiss the tomb, to be close to something sacred. Today we have a wider view of what is sacred, one that does not negate the focus of the religious believer on special places of holiness, but shifts the vision to see the natural world with new eyes. Nature is itself sacred.

THE SACREDNESS OF THE WILD

We have become aware of the spiritual value of nature, the sacredness of the wild, of places we must revere and protect for their own sake. As we walk, through whatever landscape, we take notice of the physicality of things, for physical things also have their spiritual dimension. This, like the pilgrim touching the tomb of the saint with reverence, will involve us touching the world as we pass, appreciating its solidity and presence. We climb a stile over a stone wall into a field, and instead of clambering over quickly we lay a hand on the topmost stone and feel its texture, sharp slate or rugged granite; we experience for a moment its temperature. We admire a tree, then feel its bole, pat and stroke the bark in recognition of another living being. We run our hand over a clump of moss and, touching, find it filled with this morning's rain. Mindfulness through touch.

The Long-distance
Walk

Have you ever thought of tackling a really long walk – a walk that takes over and becomes your life, transporting you way beyond the horizon? Many of us will probably admit to dreaming that one day, equipped with a small backpack and comfortable boots, we will set off on such an adventurous hike. The daily walk is one thing – the sort taken by Charles Darwin on his 'sandwalk' around the peripheries of his large garden, or the walk we make through the park, down a country lane or though local woodland – a walk that brings us home by nightfall. Such familiar routes offer a great opportunity for practising mindfulness and improving our health, mental and physical. But the long-distance walk is something else.

59

We can enjoy such walks vicariously, by reading the journals of those who have accomplished them, while still dreaming of our own tentative future plans. Robyn Davidson records one such journey in her book *Tracks*; she walked over two thousand miles with a dog and three camels from Alice Springs in the great Red Centre of Australia, through the Gibson Desert, to the Indian Ocean. Feeling alternately elated with buoyant confidence or very small and very alone, it became as much an inner journey as it was an exploration of the dry and empty landscape of desert and bush. Another favourite of mine is *Between the Woods and the Water* by Patrick Leigh Fermor, telling part of his mammoth trek across Europe in the 1930s from London to Constantinople; I am still haunted by his description of the Great Hungarian Plain.

HORIZON TO HORIZON

The latest book to astonish me, with its vivid account of an awe-inspiring hike in 1868 from east to west across the United States of America, is *Afoot and Alone* by Stephen Powers. He subtitles his work '*From Sea to Sea by the Southern Route*', and attributes his journey to his love of wild adventure, asserting that tramping month after month 'is a pleasure, to be fully enjoyed only by the pedestrian.'

It is easy in everyday life to be something of a sleepwalker, to become unaware and unquestioning of the habitual patterns and routines of everyday life. It would be hard, however, to be a sleepwalker on a long-distance walk that takes one from horizon to horizon, day after day, transporting you to new worlds. There are changes to be seen in the local wildlife as one leaves one natural habitat for another, and changes to the human landscape when walking from village to town to countryside, with intimations of historical events peculiar to particular places. There are also internal changes within the walker, as Robyn Davidson found in her long trek across Australia, finding that she was able to sort out some aspects of her life that had been troubling her.

THROUGH A WEARY FOOTMAN, GREETING

Stephen Powers walked across America just after the countryside and the population had been devastated by the Civil War; attitudes to Yankees and Confederates were still bitter and raw, while the shadow of General Sherman lay heavily across the southern states. Powers' use of language, when describing people, whether landowners or freedmen, Mexicans or Native Americans, reflects the prejudices of the era, jolting the modern reader (but no less worth reading for all that). Society was just beginning to reassess its attitude to slavery. Powers finds tremendous poverty among the poor whites, and discovers that a man with a large property treats his hired freedmen better than the man with a small holding. He is perplexed when entering the mansions of Confederate landowners to find them carpet-less; investigation reveals that so many soldiers died thereabouts that, for hasty burials, carpets had to do for coffins. Civil war is gut-wrenchingly painful.

This is what mindfulness is about – becoming more aware of ourselves and our surroundings, questioning the society we live in and its history, finding who we are as we make our various journeys through the world.

Powers tramps westward with the sun through pine forests and over mountain passes, across vast plains and scorching deserts; he is observant and has a good eye for the wildlife. On reaching the west coast, the fine chirruping of hummingbirds fascinates him and he is intrigued to watch a Californian woodpecker drilling holes in a tree in which to stash its acorns. Finally, he dips his hand into the sea by the Golden Gate and says: 'The Sunrise to the Sunset Sea, through a weary footman, Greeting.'

A Walk with the
Moon and **Stars**

A great time for a long walk is in the evening, when we
can share the landscape of the countryside, or the urban
scene of the city, with the setting of the sun and the
coming of twilight; we observe the changing colours
of the sky until, darkening, it begins to reveal the stars.
Maybe there is also a moon.

As we walk, the heavens may trigger in us a troubling
sense of our insignificance, our smallness in the face of
the vast and ancient universe and the utter irrelevance
of our short lives, or else they might inspire in us a calm
sense of wonder. It all depends on how we think about it.

St Frances of Assisi, in the thirteenth century, offered a comforting vision of the heavens in his famous 'Canticle of the Creatures'. In the canticle he praises his God or Brother Sun and Brother Wind, for Sister Water and Mother Earth. It also includes the line: 'Be praised, my Lord, through Sister Moon and all the Stars; You have made the sky shine in their lovely light.' It comes as no surprise to learn that in 1979 he was declared patron saint of ecology by the Roman Catholic Church.

But can we draw comfort from the cosmos?

OUR PLACE ON THE PLANET

The sun itself is enough to make us feel small; at a million times the volume of the Earth, that fiery furnace – converting four million tons of its mass into light and heat every second, as it has done for over four billion years – is the star we know best. As it sets, its light is somewhat subdued and reddened by the atmosphere; we are able to contemplate what we owe to that great ball of nuclear energy, the essential powerhouse of the evolution of life on our planet. As it slips beneath the western horizon we may then turn to the east and observe the lilac shadow of our world rising up into the stratosphere, a prelude to the darkness that will reveal the stars.

Walking through twilight from daylight into darkness is a great time to be mindful of our place on the planet as it rolls towards the east through space, turning daily on its axis. For a moment we may imagine ourselves as viewed by a handful of astronauts from the moon – inhabitants of a blue and white bauble, a tiny world far from the sun, suspended in emptiness.

WE OWE ALL THIS TO THE STARS

The stars appear. If we are walking on a summer's evening and we live in the northern hemisphere, we will see the summer triangle of bright stars: Deneb in Cygnus the Swan, Vega in Lyra the Lyre and Altair in Aquila the Eagle. If the sky is really clear, without light pollution, we may be treated to a great view of the Milky Way running down to the southern horizon, a haze of millions of stars, all of them suns – many much bigger than our own local sun. And if we were to stop and contemplate their distances, they would undoubtedly challenge our powers of thinking.

But it is what stars do that matters to us. They may seem remote to our lives, shining at unimaginable distances from the solar system, but in reality our relationship with them is intimate. In the early stages of this universe there were none of the atoms essential for the evolution of life – carbon, nitrogen, oxygen, calcium, sodium, potassium, iron and so forth. The universe then was composed mostly of hydrogen and helium. The more complex atoms, those needed for building plants and people, had to be forged from the simpler hydrogen and helium – and the only place such nuclear alchemy can take place is in the heart of massive stars. It was only when those stars exploded at the end of their careers that the universe was seeded

with the chemistry of life. After billions of years
the solar system was formed, the sun with its planets,
including Earth. Evolution could begin. Our birth was
long in its gestation.

As we walk in the dark, perhaps along a familiar path,
eschewing the use of a torch, we are aware of the trees
overhead, silhouettes of branches through which the
stars twinkle; an owl hoots from woodland; our nostrils
are assailed by the smell of new-mown hay; we breathe
in and out mindfully, tasting the night air. We owe all
this to the stars. Without them we would not be here.

The
Creative Power
of Walking

The benefits that come from going for a good walk
are fairly obvious: it gets the body moving, exercising
and strengthening the legs; it strengthens the heart
and gets the blood pumping round your system;
it deepens the breathing and opens your
lungs to refreshing air. It offers a very
effective way to practise mindfulness,
to find peace in the present moment.
But another benefit is not often
mentioned – it can also be a very
creative exercise.

The creativeness of walking is celebrated in Australian Aboriginal myth. The first migrants to the continent, fifty thousand years ago, walked deep into the interior, from rock outcrop to billabong, from salt pan to dry river bed, through a blistering red landscape dotted with tufts of dry white spinifex, weaving their way through wattle, thorn bush and spear-like desert oak. Snakes hid in the sand, and in the deep blue sky shoals of green budgerigars converged on waterholes. The Aborigines recorded their journeys in song as a way of map-making, identifying the features of that extraordinary wilderness so that others could follow the path. These were the songlines, the invisible pathways that criss-cross Australia, pathways that the ancestors walked in the beginning. In Aboriginal memory, this all took place in the Dreamtime, when the ancestors are believed to have created the land by singing it into existence. According to this mythical way of thinking, the singer, the song and the path are all one; the first people created the land by being there, seeing it for the first time and walking to its horizons.

A PHILOSOPHICAL CONUNDRUM

Dig deep into a myth that has stood the test of time and we come to a truth clothed in the form of a story or an image. The Dreamtime songlines suggest that we have a creative relationship with the country we walk through, and in a real sense we create what we see by looking and listening. We can never be detached observers. There is an old philosophical chestnut that asks: 'When a tree falls in a forest with no one to hear it, does it make a sound?' A falling tree hitting the ground generates pressure waves in the air, which are picked up by our ears and registered as sound by our brains. Pressure waves themselves, without the interpretation of an observer, are not sound; we create the sense of sound through our relationship with the environment, by listening.

The same is true for light and colour. There is no colour in the flowers of a spring hedgerow or a sunset sky until we, as observers, are there to 'tune in' to the various wavelengths of the electromagnetic spectrum that penetrate our eyes. Colour is the way we see these things. Without us, the concept of colour is meaningless. We bring with us not only a point of view – our position on the path as we walk – but also the way in which we register the bundles of energy that impact on our eyes and ears. We interpret the scene in our own way. Looking and listening are themselves creative activities. But what is the world like when we are not looking at it? Some philosophers have found that pondering this question can be a strangely disturbing exercise.

UNRAVELLING THE KNOT

At a more mundane level, the act of walking mindfully clears the head, making us receptive to new ideas. Many writers bear witness to the fact that when they get stuck in their writing it is often a walk that shifts the blockage. The key is to let go of the problem. This requires the same mindful exercise we use for finding peace in the present moment by focusing attention on breathing and walking. It is like relaxing a clenched muscle. In the case of a writing block, or any other mental knot that is hindering progress, we need to give some freedom to the subconscious by allowing the mind to let go. Often the solution to our problem bubbles to the surface when we are no longer struggling with it; the knot is unravelled. The walking has helped with our creativeness, getting things moving.

In every mindful walk we are also making subtle changes to ourselves – for example, allowing our attitudes to others to be more compassionate; freeing ourselves from destructive habits, thoughts or prejudices; being liberated from anxieties we have clung to for too long. Walking is a recreational activity, and we tend to forget that recreation means just that: we are recreated.

Rights of Way

We all need the wilderness; a walk in the wild is good for the human spirit, a pleasure and a therapy. Many poets and mystics have acknowledged the deep yearning we have for open spaces. The New England transcendentalist Henry David Thoreau wrote in his book *Walden: or, Life in the Woods*: 'We need the tonic of wildness.' And the Victorian poet Gerard Manley Hopkins expressed his love of the wild in the final verse of his poem 'Inversnaid':

What would the world be, once bereft
Of wet and of wildness? Let them be left,
O let them be left, wildness and wet;
Long live the weeds and the wilderness yet.

Today, there are fewer wild spaces to be left alone; there is less wilderness to cherish. The world's population has increased fourfold since Hopkins wrote those lines in 1881. Human beings are in danger of overrunning the planet, of wrecking the wilderness that we and other species all need. Our success may in the end be our undoing.

A WALK ON THE WILD SIDE

Most of our walking will be along well-trodden paths, on pavements and roads; it can be a challenging exercise to find places to walk off the beaten track where weeds flourish and nature has its way. They are worth seeking out, for they can give us a true sense of being in touch with the ground, at one with the planet.

The problem is that with a rapidly increasing world population, more and more land is tied up in private or corporate ownership, and it has required vigilance, vision and energy by our forebears to protect the wilderness for both its own sake and ours. There is something deeply unattractive about encountering, when on a country walk, a barbed wire fence across what was once open land, or a notice stating 'Trespassers will be prosecuted'. The unfortunate strain in human nature that wants total ground control over property, revealed by the need to erect 'keep out' notices, is one that itself is in need of control by society as a whole.

The world is blessed nowadays with some great national parks, vast tracts of original mountainous wilderness and forest where it is possible to walk in the wild, and the freedom to do so is both encouraged and enshrined in law. We are indebted for the existence of these open spaces, where nature can be itself, to the dedication and energy of thousands of nature lovers and conservationists worldwide lobbying for their protection.

MASS TRESPASS

The American writer Rebecca Solnit, in her erudite *Wanderlust: A History of Walking*, shares with the reader her delight at the discovery of a history of mass trespass in the UK. Public rights of way have often been closed, footpaths fenced off by unscrupulous landowners, walkers discouraged by threatening gamekeepers. Rather than give in to such bullying, some people have had the courage to challenge the closures. It was the mass trespass in the Derbyshire Peak District in the 1930s that struck Solnit most forcibly. The Peak District is an expansive wedge of open moorland between the great industrial conurbations of Sheffield and Manchester in the north of England. Labourers in the polluted cities wanted to be able to get out on a weekend into the fresh air of the countryside that was on their own doorstep, even follow old rights of way, including the track of an old Roman road that ran through the region. Kinder Scout, a millstone grit outcrop of the Pennine range of hills, was a particular attraction. But they were kept out by wire, padlock and gamekeeper, forbidden to roam on the land by the owner of the property. It was only after mass trespass by local walking clubs, with the risk of jail sentences, that this intolerable situation was reversed.

Not all campaigns to protect old rights of way – or create new ones – involve breaking the law; many require the dogged and energetic dedication of a few committed people who believe in the natural human right of access to open countryside. Many of the popular long-distance walking routes in many countries around the world – ones that follow rivers from source to sea, traverse mountainous terrain, or wind along coasts – have required tedious planning and negotiation with land and property owners. Mindful of the need to keep these paths open, perhaps this offers us an opportunity, once in a while, to join a rambling club, to tramp together along a public right of way.

You Are Not Alone
in this World

Mindfulness without compassion is not true mindfulness
– and never will be. While we may be alone as we walk
mindfully, we are not isolating ourselves from the rest
of the world, ridding ourselves of the burdens and pains
born by other people. Indeed, the practice of mindfulness
should, in relaxing our self-concerns, open up the doors
of compassion towards others.

At the heart of Judeo-Christian teaching is the simple
rule always to treat others as you would like them to
treat you – to love your neighbour as yourself. Buddhism
in the East holds a very similar view, exemplified in
the Bodhisattva vow to postpone private peace in the
ultimate goal of Nirvana, until all other conscious beings

have been freed from ignorance and suffering. In both religions, it is a non-negotiable rule that other people matter and must always be cared for.

LOVING-KINDNESS

There is a meditation in Buddhism known as *Metta* (meaning loving-kindness), which involves contemplating other people in mind and heart. The purpose of the meditation is to extend feelings of love and compassion first to one's family, holding them in imagination, each individually, with their needs and problems, suffering, joys and sadness, while wishing them well. Then one widens the circle to include friends and neighbours, chance encounters, people mentioned by others in conversation, the homeless. Finally, we have to extend the same love and compassion to enemies – those who irritate us, who have put us down or even deeply hurt us. It is a demanding exercise, and resonates so well with Christian prayers of intercession that it might be better to drop the labels 'Buddhist' and 'Christian' altogether.

COMPASSION FOR REFUGES

It can be difficult to extend feelings of loving-kindness and compassion to people we don't know, but walking offers us an opportunity to identify with some of them – with refugees. We set off with the deliberate intention to dedicate, for example, this particular morning's walk to the homeless, to the foot-weary refugees of the world, trudging from country to country, continent to continent, often from poverty to poverty. The toiling families, each child holding an elder's hand and clutching a rag doll or a toy, their only possession; the old relatives bent beneath a mind-numbing load. We hold them in heart and mind for the length of our journey. Walking becomes a physical prayer or meditation.

We may not be clear about the politics of why these people are on the move, about the rights or wrongs of their predicament, whether it was economics, unemployment or fear that made them leave their homes, but they are people in pain and they call out for our compassion.

IN MIND AND HEART

For some of us, it was John Steinbeck's *The Grapes of Wrath* that made us aware of the terrible lot that befalls some people in this world, through no fault of their own. In this tale of human suffering, poor tenant farmers of Oklahoma, fleeing dust and drought in the Great Depression of the 1930s, join Highway 66, the migrant route from Mississippi to Bakersfield, California. They had been turned off their land by cold-hearted owners, or by banks and corporations who had bought up the property rights. The road west was littered with wrecks, exhausted trucks with threadbare tyres abandoned in favour of a lift or walking, the occupants sustained by false hope fed by misleading handbills proclaiming California to be a promised land, overflowing with oranges and offering plentiful work and dignity.

America's western migration is now part of history, but when we walk today we are walking at the same time, under the same sun, as millions of others toiling as refugees. These are the ones we hold in mind and heart.

Is such a walking meditation effective – does it do anything? Are such thoughts no more than the self-indulgence of the comfortable person, adopting a pitying pose? I dismiss such doubts. In the first place, it is an essential element of our own spiritual health that we learn to extend genuine feelings of loving-kindness to others, whoever they are. And then who knows what the other consequences of such a dedicated walk might be? We may be inspired to make a donation to one of the great charities who work with refugees; we may become politically active, determined to be of practical help, as many admirable people do; we may feel freer in future to challenge racist or anti-refugee remarks, ones that otherwise we might have ignored. The consequences of open-hearted meditation can be unexpected at many levels.

You Don't Have to
Conquer
the Peak

It is popular to speak of conquering a mountain, as
though the mountain itself were an adversary in need
of control. Many mountaineers speak this way, seeing
crags and precipices, peaks and distant heights as
physical challenges to overcome – which is fine, of
course. Such an approach to the difficult summits of hill
country can bring out the best in some temperaments,
develops skills and sometimes teamwork, tests fear
and encourages focus and concentration on the very
real demands of the moment. It can be dangerous
work, encouraging self-knowledge and an awareness

of one's strengths and limitations – and inevitably involves its own sort of mindfulness.

But the idea of conquering a mountain, its great bulk scoured and shaped over millions of years by the elements, wind and rain, storm and ice, seems to me to be somewhat absurd. Conquering one's own weakness or fear, perhaps – but the mountain? I imagine a cartoon of two tiny climbers, like ants, planting a miniscule flag on an Alpine peak; the mountain is quietly smiling, as if to say with a shrug, 'Oh! OK – I give in!'

THE MOUNTAIN IN THE PRESENT MOMENT

The language of conquest comes out of a philosophy of human superiority and the belief that it is our created destiny to dominate nature, to control the world and develop it for our own purposes, everything around us being there for our exclusive use and exploitation. It is a philosophy we have to question; the more mindful we become, the clearer this will be.

There are certainly times when 'getting to the top' is a worthwhile goal. The physical sense of achievement can be immensely rewarding, and the stupendous views often on offer, either looking back down the way we came or out over a jumbled landscape of undulating hills and valleys to distant horizons, can be deliciously uplifting. Sometimes we have to head for the peak and everything within us would rebel if we turned aside from the top, turned back with the challenge only half accomplished.

On most mindful walks, however, we can ignore the peak, because our intention is to become more aware of ourselves on the mountain in the present moment, to enjoy feelings of breathing and the sense of *being* on the flanks of the hill. This step we take *now* through the heather and the sedge is what matters, not straining for some imagined future state at the top of the hill.

To gain this mindful consciousness, we will sometimes have to rein in and drop those tugging ambitions to conquer the summit, but it can be hard to let go. We have to 'talk ourselves down' until we find ourselves sitting on a rock, content with the present moment and the view.

ENOUGH FOR THE MOMENT

I learned this lesson on the flanks of a dramatic and isolated peak in the north of Scotland. Suilven is a stack of ancient Torridonian sandstone, shaped by glaciations, a billion years old and standing like a gigantic cathedral on an even older bed of Lewisian gneiss. The moorland around is spotted with bogs and lochans, where red-throated divers could be seen swimming low in the water, their high haunting calls catching the mood of the wilderness.

I climbed the mountain with a friend, taking the route that goes over the saddle between two peaks. The final ascent was vertiginous and we eased our way forward and upward on all fours. The main peak of Suilven, lost in the cloud, was accessible only by a treacherous track. Should we go for it or not?

The day had been good, the views were already stupendous. I had watched a golden eagle being mobbed by two ravens, appearing intermittently out of the cloud; I had seen ring ouzels for the first time, and come face to face with rich tussocks of heather as we scrambled upwards. Enough for the moment!

JUST BE WITH THE MOUNTAIN

I know of no author who can write more beautifully about enjoying a mountain than Nan Shepherd of Aberdeen. Her love was of the Cairngorms. 'At first, mad to recover the tang of height, I made always for the summits…', she wrote in *The Living Mountain*. Later, as she came to know that great granite massif better, she records that '…often the mountain gives itself most completely when I have no destination, when I reach nowhere in particular, but have gone out merely to be with the mountain as one visits a friend with no intention but to be with him.' Adopting her attitude can improve our walk on any mountain.

Finding
Stillness
on the Way

Stillness and silence are not always what we may think they are. Stillness can be found in a jostling crowd, and silence is not always simply a lack of sound. Going for a good walk provides ample opportunity to get away from the noisy world, to leave the family (however much loved), workplace or office behind for a moment, and to explore the health-giving balm of silence, to discover what it really is and plumb some of its depths.

The English Victorian novelist Charles Dickens was one of the first to note and record the prodigious noise levels some of us are forced to bear in the modern industrialized world. His description in *Hard Times* of the incessant thumping of the steam engines (elephants 'in a state of melancholy madness'), in the mills of his imaginary, but very real, northern city of Coketown, captures the way noise can dominate and tarnish life. Today, the sounds of the city can be even worse, with the roar of aircraft rising above the rumble of traffic, the urgency of police sirens or fire engines and the wail of ambulances. At home, television and radio complete the daily cycle of noise, the background soundscape that seems to be everywhere, accompanying everything we do.

NOT ALL SILENCE IS GOLDEN

Our forebears must have taken quietness for granted in the way we tend to take breathing for granted. It was natural for them to hear only the sounds of nature while working, birdsong and the lowing of cattle, the wind and the rain, and to return to a low-lit house with only the crackling of the fire and the sound of conversation to disturb the quiet. Those days, for most of us, have gone. We have to make a conscious effort to treat ourselves to the elusive sound of silence, and to cherish it when we have found it.

Of course, not all silence is golden – there are embarrassed silences when we have 'put a foot in it' and spoken out of turn; tense silences in a fractious marriage; aggressive silences fired at us from troubled teenagers; silences from offended friends. All of these have to be handled mindfully in their own way, requiring wisdom, empathy and experience. The sound of silence we are seeking when setting off for a walk is entirely different; it is an inner thing, and not just an escape from the daily assault on our ears. We are seeking rest, and the chance to rediscover the still centre at the heart of our being.

To achieve this, there is no need to find a spot where there is a total lack of noise, where all we can hear is the numbing sound of the blood rushing through our heads. That sort of silence can be torture – and is horribly used as such in some totalitarian regimes. The silence we yearn for is achieved when external sounds – the wind in the trees, a distant dog barking – enhance rather than diminish our own sense of quietness. We have left behind us for a moment the noisy turmoil of life, and have set off mindfully to rediscover, and reconnect with, ourselves.

JUST WALK

We need to walk slowly and to find enjoyment in the simple activity of walking itself. Mindfulness can never be forced. We know what noise and clamour we have left behind and why we want to get away from it for a short period. The walking itself will help and it is good to slip into an easy, undemanding rhythm, coordinating our breathing with our steps. As the Zen Buddhist master Thich Nhat Hanh puts it in *Peace Is Every Step*, the purpose of walking is '…not in order to arrive, but just to walk.' One step after another.

As we walk, we let all external sounds become extraneous to ourselves; they are not part of our being. This is easier to accomplish in the countryside, and if we have access to the natural world then so much the better. Some solitude is helpful on a walk such as this, so that, freed from the need to communicate with others, we can begin to recognize and relish the silence within.

However, all is not lost if we live in a city and cannot immediately get away to wilder open spaces. There are innumerable opportunities in the urban environment, in parks and gardens, by rivers and canals, up quiet lanes and through cemeteries, to walk mindfully and to discover inner silence. We explore these in a separate thought.

The Fork
in the Path

You reach a fork in the path on your walk and you hesitate: which way to go? The dilemma may cause some to remember Robert Frost's 'The Road Not Taken', written in 1916 and claimed to be the best-known piece of American poetry of the twentieth century.

'Two roads diverged in a wood, and I –
I took the one less traveled by…'

The speaker in the poem is sorry that he cannot travel both the paths and contemplates looking back with a sigh, wondering what might have been if he had taken the alternative path. Regret and indecision run through the stanzas and Frost may have been having no more than a quiet dig at the indecisiveness of his friend and walking companion, the writer, Edward Thomas. Whatever Frost's original intention, however, whether serious or light-hearted, the poem struck a deep chord with the public.

THE POWER TO CHOOSE

When walking mindfully, the fork in the road will usually be of no great consequence – either way will be fine. But there is something about facing a choice that may on occasion force us to see the diverging paths as symbolic. The spirit of self-awareness that has emerged in human beings through evolution has given to us the power of free choice. This subject has been much debated over the centuries by philosophers, followed more recently by psychologists: do we really have free will or is it an illusion – all our actions already determined before we enact them, all our choices preordained? Clearly, our freedom is limited: we cannot decide to deny the laws of physics; we have inherited much of our natural behavioural traits from our ancestors; and cultural habits will have been nurtured within us by our social environment. Nevertheless, there is nothing logically false about believing that, within those limits, we have the power to choose which path to follow. And small choices may lead to huge consequences.

Mindful walking does not aim to get excited about philosophical debates, such as the problem of free will and whether we genuinely are free to choose. The purpose is to empty the mind of its daily turmoil, to find life in the present moment through focus on the breathing and, as we walk, to simply walk, one foot after the other. The aim is to be consciously awake, aware of the here and now. This gentle activity involves trusting one's inner, quieter self and letting go of problems that tie us up with too much thinking, perhaps involving work or career, relationships or family, past unresolved guilt or future risks. For the duration of the walk, we lay them to one side.

There is a creative potential in the peace this mindful walking brings, and it is sometimes experienced that a great decision comes to fruition on such a walk without trying for it. 'Of course – that's what I should do', you suddenly find yourself thinking. You return refreshed, liberated from doubt and uncertainty, a new person with a new direction. The choice at the fork in the road in your life has happened without a struggle and you move on.

THE ROLE OF 'IF'

Some choices we make in life, whether seeming small or great at the time, can, down the line, be transforming beyond prediction or imagination. There have been so many forks in the road that it is worth recollecting how we came to be here in the present moment at all. Even before we were born, chance meetings that led to marriage by ancestors changed a path in history and led eventually to our being here. If the people who became our grandparents had not met, we would never have been born. The role of 'if' is replayed throughout our own personal histories, so that if we could replay the tape of life, with all its various forks in the road, it would work out differently in every case. If we had not been ill on that occasion…if we had not met that person…if we had decided on a different career…if we had not turned down that offer…if that accident hadn't happened, and so on. Forks in the road – some faced and considered; some selected without thought; some forced upon us.

The point we come to realize is that the present moment in which we are walking, and are coming to appreciate mindfully, is unique. We are alive here, now, and may feel that the only appropriate response is one of gratitude in the face of this delicious mystery.

Walking with
Others

'Try not to walk and talk at the same time' suggests the Zen Buddhist master Thich Nhat Hanh in his book *How to Walk*. He is, of course, referring to the practice of mindful walking and not walking in general. Even so, we need to think about this injunction. Why not talk?

Anyone who belongs to a rambling group, or who has watched an untidy flock of walkers descend from the hills into a village, will know that talking is one of the great pleasures of those involved. For some, the chatter is purely social, light-hearted, jolly; for others, as in the trespassing rambles referred to in Rights of Way (see pages 76–81), the discussion may be earnestly political, driven by the eager will of activists. Either way, the walkers carry a world of conversation and ideas with them and there is a very good chance that they will not hear the breeze singing in a hawthorn bush as they pass or note the kestrel above the track. Their openness to nature will be intermittent and always interrupted. The values of walking with a group cannot be underrated but they are different from the aims of mindful walking.

THE PRIVATE QUEST FOR MINDFULNESS

The purpose of mindful walking is to learn more about oneself through quiet meditation, by focusing on the breathing, learning to dismiss wondering thoughts, letting the rhythm of walking become the conscious reality of one's experience. We become more aware of the present moment and discover how different it is from the turbulent imagined world of the head, which can dominate most of our daily activity.

We may carry a mobile phone with us for security reasons, which is fine – a wise precaution. But we should keep it switched off for the same reason that walking with other people can be a hindrance to the practice of mindfulness; even just waiting for the possible call or text message can be a nagging interruption to the exercise of self-discovery in hand. The perceived need to be in communication, all of the time, with work, friends or family, has become something of a tyrant in the modern world. We do well to take it in hand so that the technology provides a useful service and is not a taskmaster.

Another person, unlike all the other things that surround us, is another world, however well you may feel that you know them; their personal history and experience of life is different from yours and they look at the world from an alternative standpoint, unique to themselves. You can never know what it means to be them, never experience life from where they breathe. One way to understand this truth is to contemplate how you fit into their world. They cannot know what it is like to be inside your head: your world is as much a mystery to them as theirs is to you. This is why engaging with other people through conversation, whether pleasurable or not, can be a complete distraction from the private quest for mindfulness.

BRIEF ENCOUNTER

While adhering to the advice 'Try not to walk and talk at the same time', we should not miss the odd opportunity for a casual conversation with a passer-by. There can be something special and surprising about these encounters. Two people previously unknown to each other meet at a gate or by a stile; they share an enjoyment of walking and comment on the clemency of the weather or on the approaching rain. The pause for each of them is welcome and they fall into conversation. When you meet someone in this way, it is well worth being open to the encounter. They may tell you of something they have just seen that excited them – a green hairstreak butterfly, perhaps – or they might direct you to a secluded bank where orchids are in flower. You in turn may be able to tell them something about the track they face ahead. Such a meeting can be delightful and memorable. After all, people are as much part of the landscape we inhabit, the world of which we should be mindful, as are the trees and hills, butterflies or birds; the only difference is that they are immeasurably more complicated and harder to understand, carrying their own worlds within them.

A casual conversation with someone you have briefly encountered can enhance the mindful walk, and be no more a distraction than it is to walk with a close friend who shares the ability to be silent, respecting the need not to talk.

Letting Go the
Inner Turmoil

There is an often repeated story from the Buddhist scriptures about two monks on a journey. Their monastic vow included the practice of chastity, and in order to protect their virtue they were also expected never even to touch a woman.

Walking together, the two monks came to a river crossing, a ford where, although the water was not deep, the current ran fast. A young woman stood by the ford in distress, staring fearfully at the torrent. She needed to cross but didn't dare. One of the monks, mindful of her plight, took compassion on her and offered to pick her up and carry her across the flood on his back, an offer she gratefully accepted.

The monks waded across the ford, one carrying his temporary load, the other consumed with irritation, muttering and grumbling about his companion's behaviour. On reaching the far bank, the girl was deposited safe and dry and she thanked the monk profusely. The monks continued their journey, but the grumbling monk continued to mutter about how they were never supposed to touch women and what could his companion have been thinking of when he offered the girl a lift on his back? It was preposterous! This state of affairs continued for some time, until the first monk spoke: 'Brother! I put that girl down back at the ford – are you still carrying her?'

With this story in mind, we can begin to address those consuming irritations and inner turmoils that are in danger of swamping our hearts and minds, spoiling a good day, challenging our attempts to walk mindfully. Sometimes this can be far from easy.

ACKNOWLEDGE YOUR THOUGHTS

Those who practise meditation or walking mindfulness always have to deal with distracting thoughts; we recognize this as a normal state of affairs. This is why the mindful breathing exercise (see pages 28–33) is so important: it draws our attention back into the present moment and focuses on the physical activity of the body. It alerts us to the way things are in the here and now so that we begin to recognize passing thoughts for what they are, temporary flickers and agitations of the mind. Some of them can be quite trivial, like fragments of a dream. We do not have to identify with them; they are not us. They come and go like clouds, plunging us sometimes into shadow.

The advice, oft repeated ever since the days of the Buddha, is always the same. Do not fight against distracting or disturbing thoughts; that way they can become a problem. They feed on too much negative attention. The way to deal with the troubling ones is to give them space, acknowledge them: 'Ah! There is that little worry again'; and having acknowledged it, quietly dismiss it with the thought, 'Later – after I've finished this lovely walk I'll pay attention to you, give you some time.' Often, when we do this, the niggling worry is gone and can't be bothered to return – or if it does, we are better able to deal with it, our mindful exercise having eased us out of its control.

STOP AND LET GO

Deeper worries are harder to handle. Perhaps we are being undermined at work by a particular person; maybe there has been betrayal in our marriage; possibly we have done some awful thing that cannot be undone and are consumed with guilt and self-hate. Grievance and despair, fear and fury can ruin everything. We may, on a walk, sometimes catch ourselves wrapped in our troubles, arms tightly crossed, face creased and fixed, staring at the ground, oblivious to the beauty of the world about our path. We mutter an inner judgemental dialogue with employer, colleague, spouse or parent –

always trying to get the upper hand, saying what we wished we had said when the moment offered itself. None of this, of course, is productive; it neither solves the problem nor brings any spiritual peace or calm. Mindful practice calls on us to stop and let go (an exercise we may have to repeat many times).

Breathe slowly and watch the breath; relax the shoulders and open the lungs; look up at the sky, the trees, the clouds; feel pressure on the feet as the gravity of the planet gently pulls on us, holding us to the ground; smell the air, listen to the breeze, feel it on the skin; let distant sounds and birdsong penetrate into our being. However hard it may be, we have to let go the burden we are carrying. One day, when we return to the earth, we will be letting go of everything anyway – so why not start now and wake up to the glory of being alive in this special moment.

Walking by
Rivers
and Canals

We have a natural kinship and affinity with water
(see also pages 136–41) – our bodies, after all, are more
than half water – so it is no surprise to find ourselves
feeling at home and in our element when walking by
a river or canal. They are companions that stay with
us, mile after mile. They induce a sense of mindful ease;
automatically we begin to walk more slowly. These
routes have their own particular atmospheres and
support their own wildlife: a new dimension is added
to a mindful walk when we are fortunate enough to
find a good towpath or well-worn riverside track.

Canals offer a unique way in which to walk through a noisy and busy city. Once, these waterways were the highways of heavy industry; slow-moving horse-drawn barges carrying everything from coal to grain, steel to timber. Though not used as much for commerce today as when they were first dug, they thread their way through urban centres, often quietly hidden and unsuspected. To find a city canal, we need to follow the unobtrusive steps down from a bridge or wander along an unprepossessing lane by an industrial estate, perhaps at the back of a supermarket or behind an urban car park. Suddenly, you find yourself on the towpath of a quiet canal. Weeds and flowers rarely seen on the main city thoroughfares flourish by the track. Industry has made way for recreation – colourful barges, decorated with pots of flowers, are floating homes or rentable for holidays; fishermen sit quietly in absorbed peace, rods waiting to flick; swans swim lazily about on the still surface of the canal; a kingfisher may flash by. A great walk lies ahead of us, whether we turn to left or right.

A STATE OF FLUX

The river has a different dynamic: it flows. And with the flowing comes a multitude of sounds as the water swishes through reed beds, tumbles gurgling over stones, or runs rollicking down rapids to waterfalls. It is continually active, ever moving, while always the same. The structure of a river is fixed – we may trace its route on a map, note the positions of its waterfalls, follow its curves and bends – and yet it is always in the process of flowing, changing, running downhill to the sea or to a lake.

It was this quality of being fixed, while also moving, that led the early Greek philosopher Heraclitus to observe (in what became a well-known aphorism) that 'You cannot step twice into the same river, for fresh waters are always flowing in upon you.' It was his notion that everything is in a permanent state of flux, not static and unchanging, that anticipated our modern view of the world – our lives being part of a dynamic, evolving process. Change is natural.

FINDING THE ETERNAL

Walking by a river helps us to come to terms with our humanity, to be mindful of the truth that change is an essential part of our experience; life is a stream and we are mortal. In the mindful breathing exercise, by focusing on the in-breath and the out-breath we learn to let go of worries and anxieties, baggage from the past and anticipated stresses of the future. Life is here and now. So, by becoming aware of the river, we may, in peace, find something eternal about the present moment, while being conscious of the gurgling movement of the water. We also move on through our lives, we grow up and grow older every day, and yet we can find a still point at the heart of this flowing process – and be glad.

The English Lakeland poet William Wordsworth records his meditation on the eternal flow of a Cumberland stream, 'what was, and is, and will abide', in his 'Valedictory Sonnet to the River Duddon'. The Duddon is one of my own favourite rivers – I learned

as a young child to swim in its current. It is fed by
streams flowing down from the fells, from bog and
rock, bracken and heather. Gathering speed, it plunges
down into Dunnerdale between great boulders rounded
and shaped by glaciers in the last Ice Age, meandering
finally over blue-grey pebbles, down to the Irish Sea.
Wordsworth wrote:

Still glides the Stream, and shall for ever glide;
The Form remains, the Function never dies;
While we, the brave, the mighty, and the wise,
We Men, who in our morn of youth defied
The elements, must vanish; – be it so!

Exploring
the City

It would be a mistake if, living in a city, you decided that the only way to enjoy a good walk would be to flee the urban environment to find a quiet lane in the countryside. Walking through a crowded city has its own special delights and offers rich opportunities for practising mindfulness, for conscious living in the present moment, and for becoming more alert to who you are. The city does not have to be second best to the rural scene.

It is only in the last few years that human beings have become predominantly an urban species; more than fifty per cent of us on the planet now live in a built-up environment. People have moved into town to find work; the town itself moved into the country by expansion. We must look for what is good and positive in this urban growth, and for the opportunities to live mindfully.

AN UNEXPECTED RICHNESS

For our walk, we set off to find the city we inhabit, remembering that the Buddha advised 'when walking, just walk.' On every walk, we will be surprised. We might first have consulted a map to locate the nearest parks, river walks and cemeteries; identified unexplored lanes and backstreets away from the noisy thoroughfares, places not visited before. We let go of any regrets that this is not the countryside. The city can be unexpected in the richness of its flora and fauna. Urban gardens and parks contribute a wonderful wealth of flowering plants, in a density greater than we would find in many country districts, attracting bees and harbouring many species of butterfly. Cemeteries are particularly abundant in wildlife, especially if they are allowed to be a little ill-kempt, with lichen-covered tombstones showing their age. It is possible to find more species of bird here than in an average country lane.

Carry a mobile phone if you want to, but switch it off. And it may be better to go for this walk alone, letting the mind, with all its potential preoccupations, relax. It is then important to let the city speak for itself, without the distraction of having to communicate with another person. Leave that for another time.

Mindfulness first emerged as a practice in the changing society of northern India two and a half thousand years ago; new cities were growing, fuelled by a developing iron industry. The way of mindfulness held great appeal for a new generation of individuals looking for a spiritual path not dependent on the priest-dominated caste system – seekers who wanted to find their own way, without labels and free of dogma. You may feel that you are in a similar position when exploring your own city.

THE SOUNDS OF HUMANITY

When walking along the crowded city pavements, walk slowly in the rhythm of your mindful exercise (see pages 28–33). Normally we might be tempted to shove through the throng, ignoring everyone else as much as possible. But now let the people flow by as though you were paddling up a gentle stream – be aware of all the faces, all the human types – inwardly express feelings of goodwill towards them, and remind yourself that each one of them is at the centre of another world.

When you reach the park or riverbank, stop and listen to the sounds of the city, now that they are a little more distant. They are always there with us, but most of the time we expend great effort in trying to shut them out, ignoring the aeroplanes that interrupt conversation and the heavy hum of traffic as it passes by. Focus on them for the moment, recollecting that they are all the sounds of humanity, part of the symphony of a risky but exciting creation.

LOVELY EVENING!

One of the loveliest times to walk the city is at the evening hour, when people pour from offices to meet in bars and pubs, convivial and relaxed. You may make your way down to the river (a feature of many cities) to watch the changing colours on the water in the direction of sunset, ripples of almost unbelievable blue and purple and then some pink. An unexpected smidgen of a silver lining to the polluted urban air is the way the sky sometimes appears above the city, as the sun sinks behind the buildings, a ball of smouldering fire. Joggers thump past, keeping fit, and cyclists steer their way between the pedestrians on their journey home. A cautious nod to a passer-by may be greeted with a surprised 'Lovely evening!' as the usual veil of anonymity between urban strangers slips for the moment.

The Sun
on Your Back

There are still people alive today who can say 'When we were young, we looked at the sky to tell the time'. The position of the stars at night, or of the sun casting its shadows by day, was enough to fix the hour. Urban living, digital timepieces, watches and clocks have dulled this natural ability; we have become tied to the concept of precise time, for work, train and newscast. We have forgotten the sun.

Those of us who live in a temperate climate, where clouds and rain are frequent, are inclined to make comment, with surprise and pleasure, on a transitory burst of sunshine. The impermanent state of the weather is, for us, the norm and we have become accustomed to its changing patterns, even over the period of an afternoon's walk. So the sun breaking through clouds, warming our backs, can feel like a blessing and a gift, and we immediately feel grateful.

A FURNACE OF FIERY PLASMA

We seldom have time or inclination to take the thought further – to consider the sun itself, that broiling nuclear furnace of fiery plasma almost a million miles in diameter. Without it, we would simply not be here; life would never have evolved on Earth and there would be no observers to feel grateful for the sunshine. It is not surprising that people in the past were inclined to be sun worshippers; it has even been suggested that the monotheism of Jews, Christians and Muslims can be traced back over three thousand years to Egyptian beliefs in one god, the solar deity Aton or Ra. And Greek astronomers in Egypt were already aware of the enormous size of the sun, compared to the Earth, long before modern science was able to measure it.

The sun, older than the Earth, has been a constant, dependable companion to our planet for billions of years, generating the creative energy needed for the rich ecosystem that surrounds us, and of which we are a part, to grow and flourish. It has been midwife to the emergence of consciousness on Earth.

SUNRISE, SUNSET...

A way to get to know and appreciate the sun better is to make a conscious effort to notice and mentally mark where on the horizon it rises and sets, as our remote ancestors once did, season by season. A local walking route, one you follow regularly throughout the year, is ideal for this. Keep track of the sun's path as midwinter approaches and make a note of where it sets, by a distant tree, building, thorn bush or hill. Even better, perhaps, would be to get up with the dawn chorus and observe the rising sun. There is no need to erect monoliths or stone circles, as they did thousands of years ago, in order to recognize the regularity of the sun's movement across the sky and to become aware yearly of its dependable presence and the passage of time.

Sometimes, at sunset, when the sun sinking towards the horizon through fog or cloud becomes a deep red ball one can look at (though be wise and careful), you may catch the glimpse of a sunspot, a dark storm on the solar surface, and recollect that to be visible to the naked eye such an apparently tiny spot is in reality vaster in size than the world we inhabit.

A GLIMMER OF GRATITUDE

The sense of gratitude we have when the sun warms our backs – where does it come from and to what, or to whom, is it directed? Good fortune? Luck? God? The sun itself?

Teilhard de Chardin, twentieth-century palaeontologist and mystic, wrote in an essay 'The Soul of the World' (collected in *Writings in Time of War*): 'There can be no doubt that we are conscious of carrying within us something greater and more indispensable than ourselves;

something that existed before we did and could have continued to exist without us; something in which we live, and that we cannot exhaust: something that serves us but of which we are not masters…' It is to this something, I believe, that we give thanks, whether we name it or not.

One of the cardinal teachings of Buddhism is that life is characterized by impermanence; it resonates with the phrase from the Book of Common Prayer about 'this transitory life'. With the passing burst of sunshine on our back as we walk, we respond by giving thanks for the gift of the moment. We do well to catch that glimmer of gratitude, which is a lovely state to be in, and to fan its flame.

Walking in
Wet Weather

'Rain, rain, go away! Come again another day', chants the gloomy child at the window as the depressingly grey rain trickles down the glass, ruining dreams of football. The family who has planned a picnic looks anxiously up at the clouds; the organizers of an outdoor event check and recheck the weather forecast with fingers crossed. For those of us who live in places where rain is a regular but somewhat unpredictable feature of the climate, it is easy to fall into the habit of thinking of it as an irritation, a spoilsport. It is natural to do so. But the regular walker has a great opportunity to adopt a different attitude. We deepen our feelings for the world when we learn to relish the rain.

It is without doubt important to be prepared: dress sensibly and carry a waterproof when on a long hike. There is no sense in getting soaked to the skin unless a welcome hot shower is immediately available – and mindfulness is difficult to sustain when wet and shivering with cold. The aim of mindfulness is to see more clearly who we are and to understand our circumstances, to live more consciously and to dispel our inherited fog of ignorance. Cultivating a love for the rain enhances our experience of living.

THE GOLDILOCKS PLANET

Rain is one of the most valuable things in our lives, surpassing the riches of billionaires or the wealth of plutocrats. We live on a watery planet and if it were otherwise we would not be here. The evolution of life and the presence of water seem inextricably entwined, which is why scientists get so excited about the possibility of finding water on Mars. Planet Earth, with its great oceans and ice caps, roaring rivers and

freshwater lakes, drifting clouds and falling rain,
is the ideal environment for living creatures to grow
and flourish – just the right spot for conscious human
beings to emerge from their long genetic history, stand
up, and look around at the world about them with
questioning wonder.

There is a circular argument buried in here, one that
was mined by theologians in the past, some would say
faultily, to prove the existence of a divine creator. They
argued that the watery world human beings inhabited
was just right for them to prosper, and so must have
been purposefully designed by God. Added to that
was the strange fact that when water freezes, the ice
expands and floats, leaving primitive early life to survive
harsh winters at the bottom of ponds. Less religious
observers today prefer to refer to the 'Goldilocks
planet', where everything is 'just right' (neither too
hot, nor too cold; neither too wet, nor too dry) for life
to evolve, without drawing any religious conclusions
from this remarkable 'fine-tuning' of the environment.

RELISH THE RAIN

Dressed properly, and mindful of the value of the rain for all life, it becomes natural to enjoy the shower when out walking, rather than cursing it. Even as a little rain invades your defences and runs down your neck, a cold trickle beneath the waterproof, you can take it to be a pleasurable touch of reality.

Sitting on a rock eating your cheese and tomato sandwich, the rain splattering off your shoulders, you reflect with a smile that this is not a ruined day. Once you have learned to appreciate the rain as part of the life-sustaining water cycle, as important to us as the air we breathe, you begin to relish the different sorts of rain. You start to distinguish the fine mist that dampens the face or the soft rain that moistens, from the pouring rain that soaks and the sharp windblown rain that stings the flesh. You notice the large drops that fall shaken from trees as they shiver in the wet wind, or discover that what you thought was rain was spray blown back from waterfalls on coastal cliffs or in mountain gullies.

The rain is older than the sun. Those beautiful curtains you see draped and drifting across the landscape, obscuring the horizon, are the passing form taken in the moment by water that has always been present in the universe as ice, liquid or vapour. There is scientific discussion about how much of the water on Earth came to us from comets or was already there in the rocks that formed the planet four and a half billion years ago – either way, water has an ancient cosmic history, rain part of its life-giving circulation.

The Earth Beneath
Our Feet

Our walk across country has coated our boots in dirt. We try to kick and scrape it off on the road or by dragging our feet through rough grass; a piece of fencing helps to catch and dislodge some of it from the treads, but all our efforts are only partially successful. The boots will have to wait until we get home, where a scraper, scrubbing brush and water will get them clean again, ready for whatever polish or protection we use. The care for one's footwear is a major priority for any serious walker.

But as we pick and scrub away, hoping not to clog the kitchen sink and wishing we had begun the task outside, we may give little thought to the mud itself, those pieces of earth, the clay and humus, muck and soil, dead leaves and bits of grit that have clung tenaciously to our boots as we hiked over rough country. Cleaning the mud from our boots gives us a rare moment to think about the soil and the ground we walk on. We might even begin to have some respect for the dirt we wash away – we are, after all, made from the same stuff. The food we eat grows from the ground, where plants transform dirt into vegetation, and then in us the creative process goes further and consciousness emerges from the earth.

CREATION MYTHS

The earliest mythologies tell of our human links with the soil. In the Book of Genesis, Yahweh (God) moulds the first man from the earth and then breathes life into him – his name Adam is a bit of a giveaway, meaning 'earth' in Hebrew. The funeral service in the Book of Common Prayer recollects this fact with the powerful words 'Earth to earth, ashes to ashes, dust to dust'. And

Christians on Ash Wednesday sometimes have ashes smeared on their foreheads with the words: 'Remember you are but dust. And to dust you shall return.'

A less well-known Native American creation myth is told by Jicarilla Apaches and makes a similar point (the whole complex myth can be found in Joseph Campbell's landmark work of anthropology, *The Masks of God: Primitive Mythology*). The creator in this tale is the Black Hactcin, who first made animals from clay before breathing life into them, and then the birds by mixing clay with drops of rain. The story goes on to tell how the birds and animals became anxious that one day the Hactcin would leave them: 'You are not going to be with us for all time'. So they asked for a companion, a human being, someone to care for them.

Black Hactcin agreed to the request and sent the birds and animals out foraging for all the materials needed: white clay, jet, red stone, opal, red ochre, and dark clouds for hair. He then marked an outline of a man upon the ground, an outline just like himself, and put all the gathered material into it. He summoned the wind to enter the form on the ground (it left whorls on the fingertips, which are there even now, so the story tells).

Black Hactcin commanded the animals and birds not to look while this was happening – but the birds could not resist the temptation and they did look, causing things to go slightly awry, which is why human beings look so curious. Nevertheless, the birds all burst into song when the first man came alive, as they still do every morning with the dawn chorus.

CREATURES OF THE EARTH

Both the Hebrew and the Jicarilla creation myths draw attention, each in its own way, to the responsibility we have to care for the rest of creation, a matter of increasing urgency today. And they both remind us that we human beings are made from the stuff of the ground we walk on – the stuff we scrape from our boots after a long muddy walk. The soil.

There was no soil or mud on the surface of the early Earth; it has taken millions of years to create the rich fertile tilth from which plants can grow and life flourish. The grinding action of glaciers ('God's great ploughs', according to the renowned nineteenth-century geologist Louis Agassiz) reduced rock into soil, releasing a multitude of minerals. Lichens evolved that consumed more rock, transforming it into the earth into which plants could extend their roots. The mulch from trees and mosses added to the rich humus from which vegetation, animals and then human beings evolved.

We are truly creatures of the earth, close relatives of the mud that sticks to our boots.

Walking with
Elephants

We can learn something from the way an elephant walks. That may seem a strange claim – but anyone who has observed these great mammals out in the bush will recognize there is truth in it.

The discovery of locomotion was one of the great innovations in the creative process of evolution. It is something we might recollect when we go walking for pleasure, health or mindfulness. Creatures that can walk widen their horizons, for food, courtship and security; they are not tied to one spot

like other branches of the tree of life – flowers, trees or fungi. The observer walking through the African bush is always alert to movement. Ants scuttle in busy columns across the path as they forage for fodder or for aphids to enslave; lions pad quietly down to the waterhole in the evening, lethal weapons hidden away in their paws; giraffes, spotting us from above and beyond a thorn bush, lope off with long ungainly strides; the delicate legs of the antelope give them an agility and speed from a standing start that astonishes. But it is the quiet pace of an elephant that can be most surprising.

GENTLY ON THE EARTH

I was first made aware of the gentle tread of these great ear-flapping behemoths when walking in the Kenyan bush with an African guide. Just the two of us; he carried a radio in case of trouble and a decrepit-looking old gun that I doubt he had ever fired – he was bursting with confidence. The only thing that worried him was that we might stumble on a sleeping buffalo, one of the most dangerous and unpredictable beasts of the bush. We walked as quietly as we could.

'Stop', he whispered suddenly, and pointed ahead. A small herd of elephants was browsing among the thorn bushes and acacia at the edge of some forest. 'We're downwind – so safe!' We stood watching. Then a movement in the undergrowth to my right caught my attention – a colourful grey-headed bush shrike lurked there, keeping an eye on us. We observed each other for some moments and then it flew off. I turned back to watch the elephants – and they were gone.

'What happened?' I asked, perplexed. 'Maybe they heard us', he answered. Whatever the reason, they had melted silently away into the forest. Despite their great mass and enormous tree-trunk-like legs, elephants walk very gently on the earth. They disappear without fuss, no crashing or heavy thudding, none of the expected lumbering or flattening of everything around; they walk carefully. Elephants also use their feet to gently scrape the ground, dislodging grass and plants they want to eat, before curling them up to their mouths with their trunks. The foot of an elephant is a delicate, sensitive thing – what a terrible thought that years ago it was a fashion in furnishings to turn them into leather footstools with polished toenails.

A HEART-WARMING TALE

A ranch manager told me a story about the social behaviour of elephants. He had grown up on another ranch, and recalled an occasion when, on the border of their property, they had found a distressed young elephant mourning the death of its mother. She had been shot by poachers for her tusks.

They persuaded and coerced the hungry young elephant to return with them to the ranch house, where he became part of an unruly but happy menagerie of cattle and horses, dogs and people. He loved splashing in the farm dam. They fed and cared for him and over the months he grew and grew until it was decided he would be better off living with his own kind in the wild. A herd of elephants was known to be passing the ranch at the time and they delivered their charge by horsebox to where they were browsing. He trotted off without any difficulty and seemed to have no problem being accepted by the herd. The herd moved on.

Early one morning, two years later, a group of elephants mysteriously appeared, standing in silence out in the bush. A single creature emerged from the group and walked heavily towards the ranch house. He dragged a stake, his leg caught up in rolls of barbed wire and badly wounded. It was their old friend. They released him from the wire, treated his wounds and then watched as he returned to the herd, which closed ranks around him and silently melted away through the trees.

You Are a Part
of the Nature
You Walk Through

We have already begun to identify with the world that surrounds us as we walk, relishing the rain that sustains life, while inhaling the smells that come from wet ground after a shower, reminding us that ultimately we are part of the soil.

Regular walkers are privileged in enjoying a view of the world denied to many people. Walking mindfully, we naturally learn to adjust our thinking about who we are as we stroll across our own small portion of the planet's surface, down country lanes, through city streets or out into the wild. We begin to recognize our links with nature, how we fit in to the web of life that surrounds us. We who walk upright, looking about us, appreciating beauty with thoughts full of questions, are as much products of the ecosystem as are the trees, bugs, butterflies or birds. It has taken humankind a long time to understand this.

FELLOW MORTALS

This truth about the interdependence of all living things, ourselves included, is not something that each of us can work out on our own; we are dependent on hundreds of years of scientific research and upon the words of modern 'prophets' who have had the insight to see things as they are. One such prophet was John Muir, a truly extraordinary person, mountain man and wilderness sage – a mindful walker if ever there was one. He was one of the most vocal of the founding fathers of the great national parks of North America, with a particular love for Yosemite Valley in California. In his view, all other living creatures should be seen as 'fellow mortals'.

It is understandable that in the early days of humanity's evolution, men and women came to assume that they were somehow superior to nature. It was their right, they believed, to exploit and dominate the world around them, a resource provided for their own survival and pleasure. This superior view even became enshrined in the Judeo-Christian scriptures, the Book of Genesis commanding early man to 'have dominion' over all other creatures.

SAVING WILD PLACES

Muir was a Scot, born in Dunbar, who migrated with his family to Wisconsin in 1849, when he was eleven years old. He was raised by a tyrannical evangelical father, who made him learn the whole of the New Testament (and much of the Old) by heart. From the Genesis creation stories, he will have read the divine command to mankind to subdue nature and 'have dominion over the fish of the sea, and over the fowl of the air, and over every living thing that moveth upon the earth.' But as he grew older, walking through the forests of his new home, loving the trees and the birds, climbing mountains, exploring glaciers, he began to see things differently. He found another book that spoke to him of God – the book of nature.

He spoke for the wilderness, gave a voice to nature. 'In God's wilderness lies the hope of the world,' he wrote, '– the great fresh unblighted, unredeemed wilderness.' And 'In every walk with nature, one receives far more than one seeks.'

He also wrote of the human need for the wild. 'Thousands of tired, nerve-shaken, over-civilized people are beginning to find out that going to the mountains is going home; that wilderness is a necessity…' Appalled by the commerce-driven but sometimes wanton destruction of the living world, the felling of giant redwoods or the shooting of polar bears, he championed their protection. (These quotes are taken from a wonderful biography of Muir by Mary Colwell: *John Muir; The Scotsman Who Saved America's Wild Places*.)

THE PROCESS OF LIVING

As we walk, we can reflect that we share common ancestors with the trees that breathe the oxygen into the air that keeps us alive; we come from the same stock as the grain-bearing grass that gives us our daily bread. The mice and squirrels, cows and horses we encounter on our walks are close mammalian cousins. It is their world as much as ours; we belong to a joint venture.

But there is also a restlessness about nature that resonates with our own lives – always thrusting ahead, exploring new forms as it evolves. Weeds and bushes quickly take over when land is untouched, rosebay willowherb and nettles, gorse and dogwood. Life is not static, and the calm we find through mindfulness will not allow itself to become stuck in the moment. Our own lives evolve and change – it is a natural feature of the process of living.

ACKNOWLEDGEMENTS

Thanks to Monica Perdoni, my commissioning editor,
who helped me dream up the idea for this book;
to Tom Kitch for overseeing the project; to Jenni Davis
for her tactful editorial skills; and of course to the
design team at Ivy Press.